You feel bad because you're in a vicious circle

The way you feel is affected by things that happen to you, choices you make and things you've done, like the bad stuff on the opposite page. Sometimes, you can change what's happening around you, but often, you can't do much about them.

And when you allow them to affect your mood, the vicious circle kicks in and you feel worse and worse and worse…

Turn over to see how it works

I'VE LOST EVERYTHING

FRIENDS HATE ME

LOST MY JOB

I'VE LET PEOPLE DOWN

Got Dumped

Best friend blanks me

FAMILY NOT HAPPY WITH ME

ALTERED THINKING

I'VE LET EVERYONE DOWN

Got No Money

Could lose my job

GOT CRITICISED

Could lose my home

MY KIDS WILL HATE ME

BEING BULLIED

First, an event affects you

When something happens, you naturally notice it and think about it. Being sent to prison, for example, you may think "I've let everyone down". This is called **Altered Thinking.**

Altered thinking can set off a chain reaction inside you that affects the way you feel and what you do.

When your altered thinking is negative (like "I've let everyone down"), the vicious circle is triggered and you can end up really down, not getting out of bed and even feeling ill. Let's watch the vicious circle in action.

> Let's watch the Vicious Circle in action

I'VE LOST EVERYTHING

FRIENDS HATE ME

LOST MY JOB

I'VE LET PEOPLE DOWN

Got Dumped

Best friend blanked me

FAMILY NOT HAPPY WITH ME

ALTERED THINKING | **ALTERED FEELINGS**

I FEEL LOUSY

Got No Money

Could lose my job

GOT CRITICISED

COULD LOSE MY HOME

MY KIDS WILL HATE ME

BEING BULLIED

Altered thinking leads to altered feelings

If you think "I've let everyone down" you're going to feel pretty low, sad or depressed.

Maybe you feel as if you'll never get through the prison time/ bird, or you might feel depressed because you know you should have done things differently or thought about your actions and how this has affected you.

So now what happens?

Altered feelings lead to altered physical symptoms

When you feel low, stressed or emotional, you can get sweaty, tense with stomach ache or headaches. Sometimes you can feel really tired, but can't seem to get any sleep.

Your hands might feel clammy, or you get an attack of the jitters and can't sit still.

Ever had a sinking feeling or felt your heart racing? It's probably that old vicious circle spinning round!

I'VE LOST EVERYTHING

FRIENDS HATE ME

LOST MY JOB

I'VE LET PEOPLE DOWN

Got Dumped

Best friend blanked me

FAMILY NOT HAPPY WITH ME

ALTERED THINKING

ALTERED FEELINGS

LEAVE ME ALONE I'M ILL!

ALTERED BEHAVIOUR

ALTERED PHYSICAL SYMPTOMS

Got No Money

Could lose my job

GOT CRITICISED

COULD LOSE MY HOME

MY KIDS WILL HATE ME

BEING BULLIED

Altered physical symptoms lead to altered behaviour

It's only natural. You're really tired, you have a headache or maybe feeling fed up or down so you don't feel like leaving the cell, or even getting up. You steer clear of people. You don't go out on association or exercise, or don't feel like eating.

And you know what happens then? The circle goes round again, only this time, you're already ill, staying in bed and fed up, so you get even worse.

Vicious, these vicious circles, aren't they?

But there is something you can do!

Now for the *good* news! →

YOU CAN STOP THE CIRCLE!

You know the great thing about circles? They turn both ways!

In the same way that just one thing (an altered thought) led to everything else getting worse, you can start to make it better by changing one thing.

Just by eating differently or doing more exercise, or talking to someone who can understand, or changing the way you think about some things, you can affect ALL THE OTHER THINGS IN THE CIRCLE and start to feel better.

Sounds too easy? Turn over for an example.

How to stop the circle

We are going to use an example of something you may have experienced to show you how it can work.

2. This makes you feel bad – altered feelings

I feel down & scared

Oh no! 'HELP' Everyone hates me. No one will help me!

1. You've just arrived in prison and haven't been able to speak to anyone outside, staff and prisoners seem to be blanking you.

Oh no! 'HELP' Everyone hates me. No one will help me!

start here

3. You avoid other people's company – altered behaviour

I feel down & scared	I don't want to see anyone or leave the cell. I just want to be alone
Oh no! 'HELP' Everyone hates me. No one will help me!	

4. You have no energy and maybe can't sleep that night for worrying about what happened – altered physical symptoms

I feel down & scared	I don't want to see anyone or leave the cell. I just want to be alone
Oh no! 'HELP' Everyone hates me. No one will help me!	I feel tired and shattered

Now lets stop the circle!

2. You make the effort to leave your cell and find someone to talk to.

> I feel more positive, there are things I can do, people I can talk to, to get through this

> I'm not the only one going through this. Things may look different in the morning

1. You've just arrived in prison and haven't been able to speak to anyone outside, staff and prisoners seem to be blanking you.

> I'm not the only one going through this. Things may look different in the morning

start here

I feel more positive, there are things I can do, people I can talk to, to get through this	I don't feel so scared, staff and prisoners seem willing to help me.
I'm not the only one going through this. Things may look different in the morning	

3. People seem more friendly than I thought. They offer me help and support.

I feel more positive, there are things I can do, people I can talk to, to get through this	I don't feel so scared, staff and prisoners seem willing to help me.
I'm not the only one going through this. Things may look different in the morning	I feel better, more at ease

4. Although I'm in prison, things aren't as bad as I thought they would be. I will get through this!

See how it works?

THERE IS LIGHT AT THE END OF THE TUNNEL

You can take control and stop the vicious circle by changing almost anything. And it doesn't have to be a big thing!

If you manage to do something about just one thing, you'll break the vicious circle, stop it spinning down and down and start to feel better.

Try it now! Good Luck